EXTREME ANIMALS

DICTIONARY

An A to Z of the world's most incredible species

Author Clint Twist
Editorial Manager Ruth Hooper
Art Director Ali Scrivens
Art Editor Julia Harris
Production Clive Sparling
Consultant zoologist Valerie Davies
Illustrators Barry Croucher (Wildlife Art Ltd), Sandra Doyle
(Wildlife Art Ltd), Ian Jackson (Wildlife Art Ltd), Mike Rowe
(Wildlife Art Ltd), Myke Taylor (Wildlife Art Ltd), Gill Tomblin

Created and produced by
Andromeda Children's Books
An imprint of Pinwheel Ltd
Winchester House
259-269 Old Marylebone Road
London
NW1 5XJ
UK
www.pinwheel.co.uk

This edition produced in 2004 for Scholastic Inc.
Published by Tangerine Press, an imprint of Scholastic Inc.
557 Broadway, New York, NY 10012

Scholastic and Tangerine Press and associated logos are trademarks of
Scholastic Inc.

ISBN 0-439-66827-1

10 9 8 7 6 5 4 3 2 1

Printed in China

Information Icons
Throughout this dictionary there are icons next
to each entry. They give additional information
about each creature listed.

Globes
These will show you where each creature can be
found in the world. Small red dots on the globes
show where each creature is found in the world.

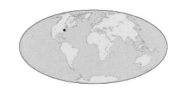

Size Comparison Pictures
Next to each entry is a symbol, either a hand or a
man showing the size of each creature in real life.

The first symbol is a human
adult's hand, which measures
about 7 inches (18 cm) from the
wrist to the tip of the longest
finger. This symbol shows the
size of the smaller creatures.

7 inches

The second symbol is an adult
human. With his arms
outstretched, his armspan
measures about 6 feet (1.8 m).
The symbol shows the size of
the larger creatures.

6 feet

EXTREME ANIMALS

DICTIONARY

An A to Z of the world's most incredible species

tangerine Press®

an imprint of

■SCHOLASTIC

www.scholastic.com

Life at the Extremes

Etruscan
shrew

The Earth provides countless opportunities for animals to make their living. Animals are everywhere—from the ocean depths to the tops of mountain ranges, and in every type of climate and condition. Life has developed an amazing variety of sizes, shapes, and abilities—even within the same basic groups of mammal, bird, fish, and insect. For example, the largest land mammal, the African bush elephant, is about 4 million times heavier than the Etruscan shrew, which is the world's smallest land mammal.

Blue whale

Physical limits

Animals grow as big as their environments allow, but there are limits. On land, the maximum size of animals is controlled mostly by the force of gravity—an animal's muscles and bones have to support its weight. In the seas and oceans, an animal's weight is supported by water, not muscle. Sea animals can grow much larger than they could on land. The blue whale, which is a sea mammal, can grow to be 13 times heavier than an African bush elephant.

Creature comforts

An animal's size is controlled by temperature also. Mammals and birds produce their own body heat. On average, they are larger than animals that rely on the environment for body heat, such as reptiles, amphibians, and fish. The blue whale, a mammal, can grow to be eight times heavier than a whale shark, which is the biggest fish in the sea. A large size works for keeping mammals warm in cold climates, but it is a problem in hot climates, where small mammals find it easier to stay cool.

Whale shark

The race for food

All animals have to eat, and most animals spend most of their time obtaining food. On land, animals that hunt and eat other animals are generally faster than animals that eat plants. Speed is a great advantage to a hunter, and it is no surprise that the fastest animal on Earth is the cheetah, a high-speed predator of the African savanna. Speed also helps the prey animals to outrun their predators.

Cheetah

Variety of Life

Leafy seadragon

Confusing the enemy

Whether it is prey or predator, it makes sense for an animal to be difficult to see. Prey animals want to be hidden from predators, and predators want to conceal their approach. Many animals combine pattern and color, such as a tiger's stripes, to help them blend into the background. But some animals go one step further, and actually imitate parts of the environment. The leafy seadragon, for example, looks just like a piece of seaweed.

Siberian tiger

Display and decoration

Animals sometimes want to be seen—especially during mating season. Some of the most spectacular sights in the animal world are meant to attract the attention of a member of the same species. The huge and exotic tail feathers of the peacock, and the high-speed dives of the peregrine falcon, are private messages. The same is true of the extremely loud territorial cries of the howler monkey.

Peacock

Hidden weapons

For many animals, life is a constant battle. Some are equipped with obvious weapons, such as the antlers of a moose, or the teeth of a saltwater crocodile. Other animals, however, rely on hidden weapons. The geographer cone shellfish defends itself against attackers (including curious humans) with a sting that injects deadly venom. The South American poraque (or electric eel) uses a completely invisible weapon in the form of high-voltage electricity.

Poraque

Endangered Animals

Some animals are naturally rare—for example, because they live only on a remote island. Many other animals, however, have become rare through damage caused by human activity. Some of this damage has been deliberate, such as hunting for meat or for furs and tusks. Some of the damage has been "accidental," such as when land is cleared for farming or road building. All rare animals, whether natural or endangered, may become extinct, and if that happens, they will be lost forever. National parks and wildlife centers provide safe places where animals can live naturally, without human interference.

Javan rhinoceros

Aa

Abingdon Island giant tortoise

Max length: 4 feet (1.2 m)

The **rarest animal** in the world is the Abingdon Island tortoise, a close relative of the Galápagos giant tortoise. The Abingdon Island tortoise is extinct in the wild, and there is only one in captivity, called Lonesome George. This elderly male tortoise is the last of his kind, and when he dies this unique species of tortoise will be completely extinct.

Max height: 13 feet 2 inches (4 m)

African bush elephant

The African bush elephant is the **largest living land animal**. It is slightly taller and heavier than its close relative, the African forest elephant. The largest recorded individual was a 13-foot (4-m) tall male that weighed more than 12 tons (tonnes). A bush elephant needs to eat up to 440 pounds (200 kg) of vegetation every day.

African Goliath frog

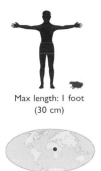

Max length: 1 foot
(30 cm)

The **largest frog** in the world is the African Goliath frog. Its body grows to a foot (30 cm) long, and its legs add at least another foot (30 cm) when fully extended. This makes a minimum total length of two feet (60 cm). A full-grown Goliath frog weighs about 8 pounds (3.6 kg).

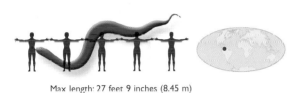

Max length: 27 feet 9 inches (8.45 m)

Anaconda

The **heaviest snake** in the world is the anaconda from the swampy tropical forests around the Amazon River. The largest anaconda on record was too big to weigh, but it measured 27 feet 9 inches (8.45 m) long, and its body circumference was 3 feet 8 inches (1.11 m). Experts estimate that this snake weighed about 500 pounds (227 kg).

Fact
An anaconda weighs about twice as much as a reticulated python of the same length.

Aa

Max length: 14 feet 9 inches (4.5 m)

Arapaima

The **longest fish** that spends its whole life in fresh water is the arapaima, which is also known as the pirarucu. Individuals up to 14 feet 9 inches (4.5 m) have been reported in South American rivers. The arapaima is long but slender, and weighs up to 440 pounds (200 kg). The rare Mekong catfish usually found in Cambodia is a shorter but heavier fish that weighs up to 670 pounds (300 kg).

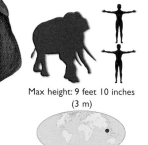

Max height: 9 feet 10 inches (3 m)

Asiatic elephant

Human beings can live to be more than 120 years old—longer than any other mammal. The next **longest-living mammal** is the Asiatic elephant, which has a normal lifespan of about 60 years. One individual that was kept in captivity in the United States lived to be 78 years old.

Max length: 65 feet (20 m)

Atlantic giant squid

The Atlantic giant squid has the **largest eyes** of any animal on Earth. Its eyes are about as big as a basketball and are bigger than the eyes of a whale. Each eye of one Atlantic giant squid that was washed ashore in Canada measured 1 foot 4 inches (40 cm) each in diameter.

Fact

Giant squid are rarely seen because they spend their lives in the ocean depths. Scientists have to study dead specimens that are washed ashore.

Australian pelican

Max height: 4 feet 6 inches (1.4 m)

The bird with the **largest beak** in the world is the Australian pelican. Its beak can measure up to 19 inches (47 cm) in length. Like most other pelicans, the Australian pelican uses its enormous beak to catch fish by scooping them from just below the water's surface. An adult can carry some of its catch back to its young in a large throat pouch attached to the lower beak.

Bb

Bald eagle

The **largest bird's nest** ever discovered was built by bald eagles in Florida in the 1960s. The original nest was built in one year by a single pair of bald eagles, but was probably enlarged by other pairs in later years. The nest was 9 feet 6 inches (2.9 m) wide and 20 feet (6 m) deep. Experts estimated that it weighed more than 2 tons (tonnes).

Max wingspan: 8 feet 3 inches (2.5 m)

Basketweave cusk-eel

Max length: 11 inches (28 cm)

The basketweave cusk-eel is the **deepest living fish**. It lives more than 5 miles (8 km) below the surface of the sea. In 1970, a research submarine caught a 6-inch (15-cm) basketweave cusk-eel in the Atlantic Ocean at the amazing depth of 27,500 feet (8,300 m).

Black mamba

Max length: 11 feet (3.4 m)

The world's **fastest snake** is the black mamba, which is equipped with a deadly venom. It can can move through the African grasslands at speeds of up to 12 mph (19 km/h) in short bursts. By comparison, the fastest speed at which a trained human athlete can run for short bursts is about 26 mph (42 km/h). How fast can you run?

Black-tailed prairie dog

Max length: 1 foot (30 cm)

The most **extensive animal homes** are built by black-tailed prairie dogs in the southwestern United States. This small rodent lives in large groups that build underground "towns" of nests and burrows. In Texas, one of the largest prairie dog towns was reportedly 25,000 sq. miles (64,000 sq. km).

Max length: 110 feet 2 inches (33.5 m)

Blue whale

The blue whale is the **largest animal** ever to live on Earth. It is several times heavier than the largest dinosaurs. Whales can grow so big because their body weight is supported by water. The largest blue whale ever caught was 110 feet 2 inches (33.5 m) long and weighed about 200 tons (tonnes). Even though it feeds on shrimp-like animals called krill, the blue whale is almost two times heavier than the largest dinosaur.

Bb
Cc

Max length: 1½ inches
(4 cm)

Brazilian wandering spider

The Brazilian wandering spider has the **deadliest venom** of any spider—strong enough to kill a human being. Its body grows to about 1½ inches (4 cm) long, with a legspan of about 5 inches (12.5 cm). Often "exported" accidentally among bananas, it is sometimes known as the banana spider.

Brown rat

Max length: 11 inches
(28 cm)

worldwide

The world's **greatest animal pest**, the brown rat, has spread around the globe by hiding in cargo on ships.

There are billions of brown rats in the world, and they eat millions of tons (tonnes) of human food each year, especially wheat and corn. The brown rat spreads disease and is making some animals extinct by eating their eggs and young.

Max wingspan: 10 feet (3 m)

California condor

The California condor is the world's **rarest bird of prey**. This magnificent bird, with a wingspan of over 10 feet (3 m), was driven almost to extinction by human activities, including hunting and farming. In the 1980s the last few wild birds were taken into captivity in an effort to save the species. Some have now been released back into the wild.

Capybara

Max length: 4 feet 3 inches (1.3 m)

The capybara is the world's **largest rodent**. An adult can weigh more than 140 pounds (62 kg) and measure up to 4 feet 3 inches (1.3 m) long. Originally, capybaras were found only along riverbanks in South America. Some were captured and raised on farms in Europe and North America. Some of these farmed capybaras have escaped and are now living in the wild.

Cheetah

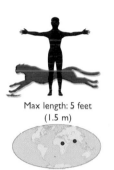

Max length: 5 feet (1.5 m)

The cheetah is the world's **fastest land animal**. It can run at speeds of up to 62 mph (100 km/h), but cannot keep this up for long. When running at top speed, a cheetah's body begins to overheat after about 15 seconds, and then it must slow down or stop. If a cheetah does not succeed in catching its prey with the first dash, the intended victim will often escape.

Fact

A fully grown but hungry cheetah can weigh as little as 50 lb (22 kg), yet it can bring down antelope that weigh much more.

Cc

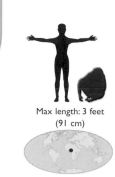

Max length: 3 feet
(91 cm)

Chimpanzee

After human beings, chimpanzees are the **most intelligent** animals on Earth. In the wild, chimpanzees often use tools to obtain food. They use stones as hammers to break open nuts, and they use thin sticks to poke insects out of holes. In captivity, some chimpanzees have learned to communicate with humans by sign language. The reason chimpanzees are so intelligent is that they are our closest relatives in the animal kingdom.

Chinese giant salamander

Max length: 5 feet 11 inches
(1.8 m)

The Chinese giant salamander is the **largest amphibian** in the world. This freshwater monster regularly reaches lengths of more than 3 feet (1 m) from nose to tail. Large individuals are now rare because this salamander is often hunted by people for food. The biggest one ever caught measured 5 feet 11 inches (1.8 m) long and weighed 143 pounds (65 kg).

Max length: ½ inch
(12 mm)

Cuban frog

The world's **smallest amphibian** is a Cuban frog with the scientific name *Eleutherodactylus limbatus*. The body of a full-grown adult male can measure as little as a third of an inch (8 mm) in length—about the thickness of a pencil. The female lays eggs that hatch directly into frogs without going through the tadpole stage.

Fact

There are two species of chimpanzee—Pan troglodytes (the ordinary chimpanzee) and Pan paniscus (known as the bonobo or pygmy chimpanzee).

Max length: 7 feet 9 inches
(2.4 m)

Dall's porpoise

The **fastest-swimming sea mammal** is Dall's porpoise, which is also known as the white-flanked porpoise. Dall's porpoise lives in the northern Pacific Ocean and can reach speeds of up to 34.5 mph (55.5 km/h) over short distances. By comparison, the fastest speed ever achieved by a human swimmer was just 5 mph (8 km/h).

Dd

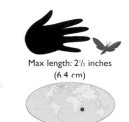

Max length: 2½ inches
(6.4 cm)

Darwin's hawk moth

The **longest tongue** of any insect belongs to Darwin's hawk moth, which lives in the tropical forests of Madagascar. This moth's tongue is much longer than its body. Normally the tongue is curled up inside the insect's mouth. When Darwin's hawk moth wants to drink nectar from deep inside tropical orchids, it unrolls its 12-inch (30-cm) tongue to reach all the way to the bottom of the flower.

Fact

Darwin's hawk moth feeds only on the nectar of an orchid called the Madagascar star, which has flowers nearly 12 inches (30 cm) deep.

Max length: 8 inch
(20 cm)

Deep-sea clam

The **slowest-growing living creature** is a clam found at the bottom of the northern Atlantic Ocean. Feeding on tiny particles of food that sink down from the surface, this mollusk takes about 100 years to reach full size.

Max length: 3 inches
(7.6 cm)

Dragonfly, Australian

The **word's fastest insect flyer** is

an Australian dragonfly with the scientific

name *Austrophlebia costalis*. When flying to intercept airborne

prey such as mosquitoes, this Australian dragonfly can reach a

maximum speed of 36 mph (58 km/h). The insect cannot keep up

this speed for more than a few seconds at a time.

Max length: 6³/₄ inches
(17 cm)

Dwarf lantern shark

The **smallest shark** in the world is the dwarf

lantern shark, which measures about 6 inches

(15 cm) long when full-grown. The lantern shark gets its

name because it has a light-producing organ on its

underside. When viewed from below, the illuminated

underside helps camouflage this fish against the

brightness of the ocean's surface.

Max length: ¹/₃ inch
(0.8 cm)

Dwarf pygmy goby

The **smallest and lightest freshwater fish** in the world

is the dwarf pygmy goby, found in the

Philippines. Adult males can measure up to a third of one

inch (8 mm) from head to tail. It takes about 7,000 of these

tiny fish to weigh one ounce (that's about 250 per gram).

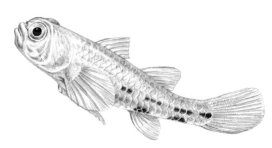

Ee

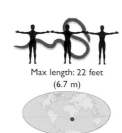

Max length: 22 feet
(6.7 m)

Earthworm

The **longest worm** to be found outside the seas and oceans is a species of African earthworm with the scientific name *Microchaetus rappi*. In the early 20th century, an earthworm measuring 22 feet (6.7 m) long when naturally extended was found in the Transvaal region of South Africa.

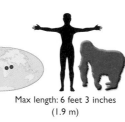

Max length: 6 feet 3 inches
(1.9 m)

Eastern lowland gorilla

The eastern lowland gorilla is the world's **largest primate**, weighing an average of 360 pounds (165 kg). An average adult male, standing upright, is approximately 5 feet 9 inches (1.75 m) tall. The lowland gorilla is slightly taller and heavier than its close relative, the mountain gorilla. Both species of gorilla are now critically endangered.

Elephant seal

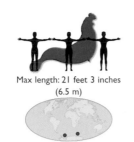

Max length: 21 feet 3 inches
(6.5 m)

The **largest seal** in the world
is the southern elephant seal. The largest
one ever recorded was an adult male 21 feet 3 inches (6.5 m) long,
weighing more than 4 tons (tonnes). Getting an accurate
measurement of the length of an adult male is difficult, because
they inflate their snouts when
angry—and nobody is brave
enough to try and
measure an angry
male elephant seal!

Emperor penguin

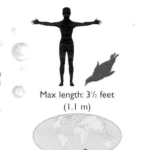

Max length: 3½ feet
(1.1 m)

No bird in the
world **dives**
deeper than the emperor penguin
when it is in search of food in the cold
waters of the Southern Ocean. When
diving to catch fish, the emperor
penguin can reach depths of up to
870 feet (265 m), and can stay beneath the
surface for more than 15 minutes.

Etruscan shrew

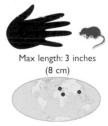

Max length: 3 inches
(8 cm)

The **smallest non-flying mammal** is the Etruscan
shrew, which is also known as Savi's white-toothed pygmy shrew.
This tiny animal lives in southern Europe, Asia, and North Africa, and
hunts insects and worms. An Etruscan shrew can measure as little as
2½ inches (6 cm) from nose to tail when full-grown, and weigh
only about one-twentieth of one ounce (1.5 g).

Ff

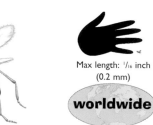

Max length: ¹/₁₆ inch
(0.2 mm)

worldwide

Fairy fly

The **smallest insect** in the world is the fairy fly, which is actually a species of wasp. These microscopic insects are smaller than some single-celled organisms. A fairy fly weighs so little that it would take about 5.7 million fairy flies to weigh an ounce (200,000 fairy flies to weigh one gram).

Flamingo

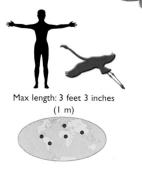

Max length: 3 feet 3 inches
(1 m)

No other bird can match the lesser flamingo for **spectacular gatherings**. Each of these brightly colored birds is about 3 feet 3 inches (1 m) tall, with large wings. Around the lakes of the African Rift Valley, where the waters are rich in shrimp, the lesser flamingo often gathers in flocks of more than 3 million birds.

Flying fox, Bismarck

Max wingspan: 5 feet 11 inches
(1.8 m)

The Bismarck flying fox of New Guinea has the **biggest wingspan** of any bat. When fully extended, the wings of a Bismarck flying fox can measure more than 5 feet 11 inches (1.8 m) from tip to tip. Despite its great size, this bat is no threat to any other living creature, because it feeds only on fruit.

Forcipomyia

Max length: ¼ inch
(0.6 mm)

worldwide

The **fastest wingbeats** of any flying creatures are those of a group of tiny insects with the scientific group name *Forcipomyia*. These insects beat their wings at an astonishing 62,760 times per minute. They have the fastest muscle movements ever measured—their wing muscles expand and contract more than 2,000 times every second.

Gg

Max length: 4 feet 3 inches
(1.3 m)

Galápagos tortoise

The world's **largest tortoises** are the giants that live in the Galápagos Islands. The largest of all is the elephant tortoise, which is found only on Indefatigable Island. One elephant tortoise that was kept in captivity grew to a length of 4 feet 3 inches (1.3 m) and weighed more than 840 pounds (380 kg).

Fact

Remote islands are good places for tortoises to develop into giants. Besides the Galápagos Islands, there are also giant tortoises on the Aldabra and Seychelle Islands.

Garden snail

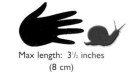

Max length: 3½ inches
(8 cm)

The world's **fastest snail** is the garden snail. When moving as fast as it can, the garden snail reaches a top speed of 55 yards per hour (50 meters per hour). If it could keep up this speed, the garden snail would take about 32 hours to travel one mile (20 hours to travel one kilometer).

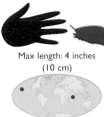

Max length: 4 inches
(10 cm)

Geographer cone

Of all the seashells in all the world, this is the one you should most avoid picking up on the beach! The geographer cone is the world's **most dangerous shellfish**. Like other cones (a type of sea snail), it can defend itself with a sharp sting that injects deadly venom. The venom of the geographer cone is strong enough to kill a person in just a few minutes.

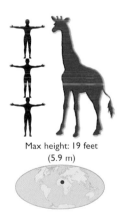

Max height: 19 feet
(5.9 m)

Giraffe

The world's **tallest animal** is the giraffe. With long legs and a very long neck, these unique animals average about 16 feet 5 inches (5 m) tall when full-grown. The tallest giraffe on record was a male that reached the amazing height of 19 feet (5.88 m). Giraffes use their short horns as weapons. Their long necks give these animals a dangerously long reach.

Gg

Max length: 1¾ inches
(4.4 cm)

Golden poison-arrow frog

The **deadliest toxin** produced by any animal is produced by the golden poison-arrow frog. The toxin is produced by special glands in the frog's skin, so its whole body is covered by a thin layer of poison. The toxin is so deadly that just touching one of these frogs with bare hands is enough to kill a person.

Fact

Native peoples in the tropical forests of Central and South America use frog toxins to make their darts and arrows into more effective hunting weapons.

Max length: 1¾ inches
(4.4 cm)

Golden silk spider

The world's **largest webs** are made by golden silk spiders in tropical rain forests. Their huge webs can measure up to 10 feet (3 m) across, and are strong enough to trap small birds. The golden silk spider gets its name from its web, which has a distinct yellow color that glitters like gold in sunlight.

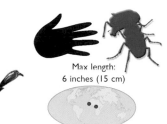

Max length:
6 inches (15 cm)

Goliath beetle

The **heaviest insect** in the world is the Goliath beetle from the rainforests of Africa. An adult male can weigh up to 3½ ounces (100 g) and measure more than 4 inches (10 cm) in length. Male Goliath beetles use their horns to fight each other in fierce battles over territory.

Max length: 11 inches (28 cm)

Goliath bird-eating spider

The **biggest spider** in the world is the Goliath bird-eating spider, from the coastal forests of Venezuela and Guyana. The largest one ever found had a legspan of 11 inches (28 cm). Bird-eating spiders do not make webs—they hunt prey on the ground, in trees, and on the forest floor.

Hh

 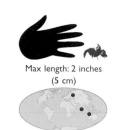

Max length: 2 inches
(5 cm)

Harlequin shrimp

Coral reefs are very colorful, and so are many of their inhabitants. The prize for the **most colorful** of all goes to the harlequin shrimp, which is also known as the clown shrimp. In addition to its bright colors, this animal also has unusual front legs that are flattened like paddles. The 2-inch (5-cm) long harlequin shrimp hides in crevices during the day, and comes out at night to feed.

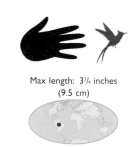

Fact
The only food that harlequin shrimp in the Red Sea and the Indian Ocean will eat is the feet of starfish.

Max length: 3¾ inches
(9.5 cm)

Horned sungem

No bird flaps its **wings faster** than the horned sungem. This South American bird can achieve 90 wing beats per second when it is hovering to drink nectar from rainforest flowers. A wingbeat is one complete up-and-down movement, which means that the horned sungem moves its wing muscles at a rate of more than 10,000 times per minute.

Howler monkey

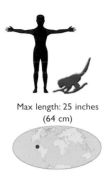

Max length: 25 inches
(64 cm)

Howler monkeys have **louder voices** than any other land animal, and the red howler monkey is the loudest of them all. This monkey can be heard more than 3 miles (5 km) away. Howler monkeys are slow-moving, and live in groups in the upper branches of rainforest trees. They use their voices to separate their territory from that of their neighbors.

Hummingbird, Bee

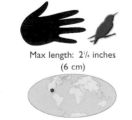

Max length: 2¼ inches
(6 cm)

The **smallest bird** in the world is the bee hummingbird from Cuba. This tiny bird has a total length of only 2¼ inches (6 cm) when full-grown. It weighs only 0.06 ounces (1.6 g), which is about the same as an average butterfly. The bee hummingbird's eggs are only about a quarter of one inch (6 mm) long.

Ii

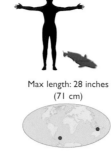

Max length: 28 inches
(71 cm)

Icefish

All fish are cold-blooded animals, but none has **colder blood** than the icefish, which live in the seas around Antarctica. The 23 species of icefish all have a natural antifreeze in their blood that allows them to withstand temperatures as low as 32°F (0°C), which would kill other fish.

Fact

Warm-blooded animals (mammals and birds) can survive short periods of sub-zero temperature because their bodies produce their own heat.

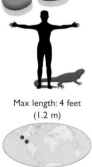

Max length: 4 feet
(1.2 m)

Iguana, spiny-tailed

The spiny-tailed iguana is the **fastest reptile** in the world. It lives in the forests of Central America and feeds on insects and worms. The spiny-tailed iguana is itself hunted by birds of prey, and it can reach speeds of up to 21.7 mph (39.4 km/h) when trying to escape one of these flying predators.

Illacme plenipes

Max length: 12 inches
(30 cm)

Illacme plenipes is the scientific name for the millipede which has **more legs than any other animal**. The word millipede means "thousand legs," but no animal has quite that many. The record is 750 legs (375 pairs) on a specimen of the *Illacme plenipes* millipede that was found in California.

Japanese spider crab

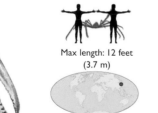

Max length: 12 feet
(3.7 m)

No crustacean on Earth has **longer legs** than the Japanese spider crab. Its body is about one foot (30 cm) across when full-grown, but its giant claws can grow to be more than 12 feet (3.7 m) from tip to tip. The Japanese spider crab lives in deep water and uses its enormous claws to collect food from the sea bottom.

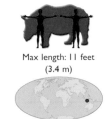

Max length: 11 feet
(3.4 m)

Javan rhinoceros

All species of rhinoceros are **rare and endangered** because they are hunted for their unique horns. The Javan rhinoceros is the rarest of them all, and has been hunted almost to extinction. There are fewer than 70 of these large, timid creatures still living wild in the forests of Southeast Asia.

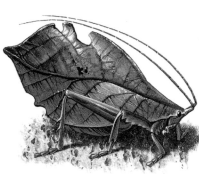

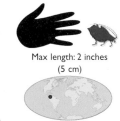

Max length: 2 inches
(5 cm)

Katydid

The dead-leaf katydid has the **best camouflage** of any insect. It is related to grasshoppers and crickets, and lives in the rainforests of eastern Peru. Its wings are colored and shaped exactly like a dead leaf. When it is resting on a branch, the dead-leaf katydid becomes almost invisible to insect-eating birds and other predators.

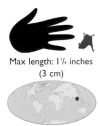

Max length: 1¼ inches
(3 cm)

Kitti's hog-nosed bat

The world's **smallest mammal** is Kitti's hog-nosed bat, which is also known as the bumblebee bat. This tiny animal is found only in a few caves in Thailand. When full-grown, this bat measures about 1¼ inches (3 cm) long, but has a wingspan of about 5 inches (13 cm). It weighs about one-fourteenth of an ounce (2 g).

Max length: 10 feet (3 m)

Komodo dragon

The **biggest lizard** in the world is the Komodo dragon, a species of monitor lizard that is found only on a few Indonesian islands. The Komodo dragon can grow to 10 feet (3 m) in length and weigh up to 365 pounds (166 kg). This huge lizard has a fearsome reputation and is reported to have killed and eaten cattle and human beings.

Kk
Ll

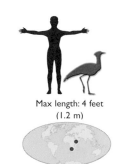

Max length: 4 feet
(1.2 m)

Kori bustard

The Kori bustard, which is also known as the paauw, is the **heaviest bird** that is able to fly. An adult can weigh as much as 42 pounds (19 kg) yet still manage to take off and fly. If these birds grow any heavier, they remain stuck on the ground and become easy victims for predators.

Fact
The four species of freshwater lungfish are distantly related to the coelacanths—the "living fossils" of the ocean depths.

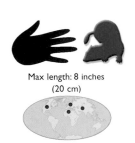

Max length: 8 inches
(20 cm)

Least weasel

The **smallest meat-eating mammal** in the world is the least weasel, which is also known as the dwarf weasel. This small predator measures no more than 8 inches (20 cm) from head to tail, and weighs a maximum of 2¹/₂ ounces (70 g). The least weasel is a ferocious hunter of mice, lizards, and small birds, and consumes about one-third of its own body weight each day.

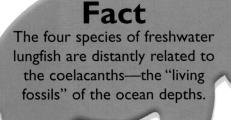

Max length: 8 feet 4 inches
(2.5 m)

Leatherback turtle

The leatherback turtle is the **biggest of all the seagoing turtles**, and is the largest member of the tortoise family. An adult male can measure up to 8 feet 4 inches (2.5 m) in length, and weigh more than 1,200 pounds (540 kg). The leatherback turtle spends most of its time in the open ocean, where it feeds mainly on jellyfish.

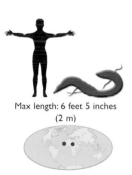

Max length: 6 feet 5 inches
(2 m)

Lungfish

Most fish can live for only a minute or two out of water—they soon die from lack of oxygen because their gills cannot breathe air. The lungfish is different—it is a **fish that can breathe out of water**! When its freshwater swamp habitat dries out, the lungfish burrows deep into the mud. It can stay alive for up to four years because it can breathe air through a pair of simple lungs.

Mm

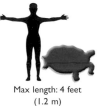

Max length: 4 feet
(1.2 m)

Marion's Tortoise

The **greatest age** of any land animal is 152 years, achieved by a male Marion's tortoise from the Seychelles Islands in the Indian Ocean. One that was captured from the wild in 1788 lived in captivity until 1918. This animal might have lived even longer, because it didn't die of old age—it was accidentally killed by its keeper.

Max length: 4 feet 6 inches
(1.4 m)

Mexican beaded lizard

The Mexican beaded lizard is one of only two species of lizard that can deliver a **venomous bite**. The other venomous lizard is the closely related gila monster. Both of these lizards live in desert habitats, and feed on birds and small mammals. The Mexican beaded lizard can give a person a very painful bite, but such bites rarely result in death.

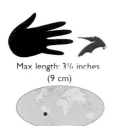

Max length: 3¾ inches (9 cm)

Mexican free-tailed bat

The Mexican free tailed bat **gathers in larger numbers** than any other wild mammal. During their annual migration, up to 20 million of these small bats can be found in a single cave in Texas. Free-tailed bats were given their name because their tails are thin like those of mice, rather than enclosed in a wide membrane like the tails of most bats.

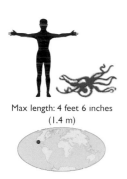

Max length: 4 feet 6 inches (1.4 m)

Midgardia xandros

The **biggest starfish** in the world has the scientific name *Midgardia xandros*. One found on the sea bottom in the Gulf of Mexico measured 4 feet 6 inches (1.4 m) across its arms from tip to tip. *Midgardia xandros* is very fragile, and its long arms easily break away from the central body, which is only about one inch (2.5 cm) in diameter.

Mm

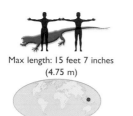

Max length: 15 feet 7 inches
(4.75 m)

Monitor

The world's **longest lizard** is the Salvadori monitor from the large, tropical island of New Guinea. This slender relative of the Komodo dragon can reach a total length of 15 feet 7 inches (4.75 m). Nearly three-quarters of the Salvadori monitor's length is made up of its extremely long, whiplike tail.

Fact

The Salvadori monitor is often called the tree monitor because it is an agile climber that hunts birds and small lizards among the branches.

Max length: 11 feet 6 inches
(3.5 m)

Moose

The **largest of the world's deer species** is the Alaskan moose. Males can measure 11 feet 6 inches (3.5 m) in length, and weigh more than 1,800 pounds (816 kg). The moose, known as the elk in Europe, has the largest antlers of any deer. The antlers of one Alaskan bull moose measured 6 feet 6 inches (199 cm) from tip to tip.

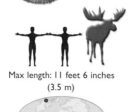

Namaqua dwarf adder

The **smallest venomous snake** in the world is the Namaqua dwarf adder from Namibia, in southern Africa. It is also known as Schneider's puff adder. When full-grown, these snakes measure about 8 inches (20 cm) in length. The Namaqua dwarf adder spends most of its time burrowed beneath sandy soil, waiting to ambush its prey of small mammals and birds.

Max length: 8 inches (20 cm)

North Atlantic lobster

Max length: 3 feet 3 inches (1 m)

The world's **heaviest crustacean** is the North Atlantic lobster, also known as the American lobster. One caught near the coast of Canada in the 1970s weighed just over 44 pounds (20 kg), and measured 3 feet 3 inches (1 m) in length. Lobsters of this size are now extremely rare because of overfishing.

Northern pygmy mouse

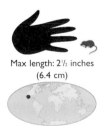

Max length: 2½ inches (6.4 cm)

The northern pygmy mouse of Mexico and the southwestern United States is the **smallest rodent** in the world. When full-grown, it measures no more than 4½ inches (11 cm) from nose to tail, with a body length of just 2½ inches (6.4 cm). The northern pygmy mouse can weigh as little as a quarter of an ounce (7 g).

Oo

Ocean sunfish

The **greatest egg producer** in the world is the ocean sunfish, which rarely comes within sight of land. A single female sunfish can lay up to 300 million eggs at a time. The ocean sunfish is also the world's largest bony fish. A full-grown adult measures more than 12 feet (3.7 m) in length, and weighs more than 4,500 pounds (2,000 kg).

Max height: 9¼ feet (2.8 m)

Ostrich

The **largest bird** in the world is the flightless ostrich from North Africa. The largest males are 9 feet 3 inches (2.8 m) tall and weigh up to 350 pounds (160 kg). The ostrich also produces the world's largest eggs. The average ostrich egg measures about 8 inches (20 cm) in length and weighs about 3¾ pounds (1.7 kg).

Max length: 0.01 inches
(0.4 mm)

Patu digua

The world's **smallest known spider** has the scientific name *Patu digua*. It was discovered in the forests of Borneo in the 1970s. When full-grown, the *Patu digua*'s body length is about fifteen-thousandths of an inch (0.37 mm), which is much smaller than the period at the end of this sentence.

Fact

Strictly speaking, the peafowl is not a wild animal—it was domesticated as a food animal thousands of years ago.

Max tail span: 10 feet
(3 m)

Peafowl

The **most extravagant display** in the whole animal kingdom is made by the male peafowl (peacock) when it raises its spectacular train of some 150 large feathers from its lower back. When fully raised, a peacock's train measures about 10 feet (3 m) across. The "eye" at the end of each train feather is intended to attract the attention of the female peafowl.

Pp

Pp

Max length: 1 foot 8 inches
(51 cm)

worldwide

Peregrine falcon

The world's **fastest bird**, and the fastest living creature, is the peregrine falcon. This bird of prey can fly at the amazing speed of 100 mph (161 km/h). It flies fastest at the bottom of steep dives reaching speeds of over 200 mph (322 km/h). The bird rarely uses such speed when it hunts. It saves its maximum performance for displays over its territory.

Max length: 1 foot 1 inch
(33 cm)

Piranha

The most **dangerous freshwater fish** is the piranha, which is found in some South American rivers. It is a small, carnivorous fish about 8 inches (20 cm) long, that lives in schools of more than 100. A school of hungry piranha can strip the flesh from an unlucky horse (or a human being) in a few minutes, leaving only the bones.

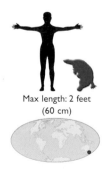

Max length: 2 feet
(60 cm)

Platypus

The world's **weirdest mammal** is the platypus, which is found in some Australian rivers. The platypus has a ducklike bill, a beaver-like tail, and poisonous claws on its feet. But the strangest thing is that the females lay eggs rather than giving birth to live young. The platypus is one of only three mammals that lay eggs.

Poraque

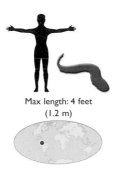

Max length: 4 feet
(1.2 m)

Several species of fish can discharge electricity—either to stun their prey or to defend themselves. The **biggest natural electric shock** is delivered by the poraque, a South American freshwater fish that is often mistakenly called an electric eel. The poraque can shock an unwary swimmer with up to 650 volts, enough to stun an adult human.

Pronghorn

Max length: 5 feet
(1.5 m)

The pronghorn antelope is the **world's fastest animal over medium to long distances**. It can run for more than 3 miles (5 km) at an average speed of 35 mph (56 km/h). It uses its speed and stamina to get away from predators such as the puma, but it is not fast enough to escape human hunters in off-road vehicles.

Pp Qq

Max length: 2½ inches
(6 cm)

Pygmy mouse lemur

The **smallest primate** discovered so far is the pygmy mouse lemur, from the tropical forests of Madagascar. When full-grown its body is only about 2.5 inches (6 cm) long, with a 5-inch (12.5-cm) tail. The pygmy mouse lemur weighs about one ounce (28 g).

Max length: 11 inches
(28 cm)

Queen Alexandra's birdwing butterfly

The world's **biggest butterfly** is Queen Alexandra's birdwing, which is found only in the tropical forests of New Guinea. This magnificent insect can have a wingspan of more than 11 inches (27.5 cm). It has become a prize target for collectors and this butterfly is now strictly protected by law.

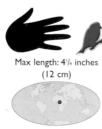

Max length: 4¼ inches
(12 cm)

Quelea, red-billed

The **largest concentration of birds** ever recorded was a roost of red-billed queleas in Sudan, which contained about 32 million birds. The red-billed quelea is a seed-eater that has become a serious pest for grain farmers in Africa. A flock of millions of queleas can completely devastate an entire region's harvest.

Rattlesnake, eastern diamondback

Max length: 8 feet 2 inches (2.5 m)

The **largest rattlesnake** is the eastern diamondback, which is also the world's heaviest venomous snake. When full-grown, it can weigh up to 34 pounds (15 kg), while it measures less than 8 feet 2 inches (2.5 m) long. An eastern diamondback weighs about twice as much as a king cobra of the same length.

Red kangaroo

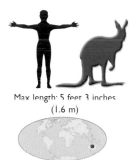

Max length: 5 feet 3 inches (1.6 m)

The **largest marsupial** in the world is the red kangaroo that lives in the dry landscapes of central Australia. An adult male is about 5 feet (1.5 m) tall, with a tail about 4 feet (1.2 m) long. Red kangaroos live in small groups of about 4 to 10 animals. When threatened by predators such as dingoes, they can bound away at speeds of up to 30 mph (50 km/h).

Rr

Max length: 33 feet
(10 m)

Reticulated python

The world's **longest snake** is the Asian reticulated python, which barely pushes the South American anaconda into second place. The largest reticulated python on record measured 33 feet (10 m) in length, and was found on the Indonesian island of Celebes. Like the anaconda, the reticulated python is a constrictor that kills its prey by suffocation.

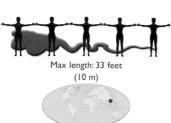

Fact
Other locust species are still very much alive in parts of Africa and Asia, and they often form swarms of more than a billion insects.

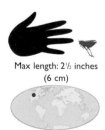

Max length: 2½ inches
(6 cm)

Rocky Mountain locust

The **largest insect swarm** ever seen was made in the 19th century by the now-extinct Rocky Mountain locust. In 1874, a swarm containing more than 12 trillion of these insects flew over Nebraska, in the U.S. The swarm covered an area of about 193,000 square miles (500,000 sq. km) and weighed more than 20 million tons (tonnes).

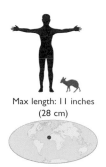

Max length: 11 inches
(28 cm)

Royal antelope

The **smallest antelope** in the world is the royal antelope, from the tropical forests of West Africa. When full-grown, this tiny antelope stands only about 11 inches (27 cm) at the shoulder, and weighs about 7.5 pounds (3.3 kg), about the same as a domestic cat.

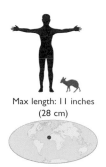

Ruppell's vulture

Max wingspan: 8 feet 4
inches (2.55 m)

The world's **highest-flying bird** is Ruppell's vulture. One specimen collided with a jet aircraft at an altitude of more than 37,000 feet (11,300 m) above West Africa. Vultures often fly high in order to spot the dead animals on which they feed, but they usually fly no higher than about 20,000 feet (6,100 m).

Ss

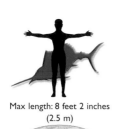

Max length: 8 feet 2 inches
(2.5 m)

Sailfish

The **fastest swimmer in the sea** is the sailfish. This large, ocean-going fish can travel through the water at a speed of more than 62 mph (100 km/h) over short distances. This incredible speed is produced by special muscles that are used only for high-speed swimming. For ordinary swimming, the sailfish uses its normal muscles.

Max length: 28 feet
(8.5 m)

Saltwater crocodile

The world's **largest reptile** is the saltwater crocodile, which is also known as the estuarine crocodile. This massive predator lives around the coastlines of Southeast Asia and Australasia. An adult saltwater crocodile can reach a length of up to 28 feet (8.5 m) and can easily seize prey as large as a human being.

Seadragon, leafy

Max length: 1 foot 6 inches (46 cm)

The award for the **best fish camouflage** is held by the leafy seadragon, which is a species of seahorse. It lives on coral reefs, and spends most of its time hiding among seaweed. The body of the leafy seadragon has a number of long, ragged flaps that help it blend in with the seaweed.

Max length: 68 feet (20.7 m)

worldwide

Sperm whale

All whales can dive deep below the ocean surface, but the sperm whale **dives deepest** of all. When hunting for its favorite food, deep-sea squid, a sperm whale can reach depths of more than 8,200 feet (2,500 m). It can stay underwater for nearly two hours before coming to the surface to breathe.

Ss

Max length: 5.5 inches
(14 cm)

Spine-tailed swift

The world's **fastest bird in level flight** is the spine-tailed swift, which is also known as the white-throated needletail. When flying horizontally, it can reach a maximum speed of 106 mph (170 km/h). Although the peregrine falcon can dive at much faster speeds with the help of gravity, it cannot beat the spine-tailed swift in level flight.

Fact
Contrary to popular belief, swifts are not closely related to swallows—their closest relatives are, in fact, hummingbirds.

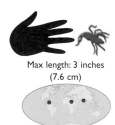

Max length: 3 inches
(7.6 cm)

Sunspider

The world's **fastest-moving spiders** are the sunspiders, which are also known as wind scorpions. Sunspiders are not really spiders, but are close relatives of both spiders and scorpions. They are desert creatures, and at night they hunt prey by racing across the sands at speeds of more than 10 mph (16 km/h).

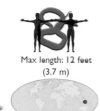

Max length: 12 feet
(3.7 m)

Taipan, inland

The world's **deadliest land snake** is the inland taipan from northeastern Australia. A single inland taipan carries a tiny amount of venom in its poison glands—about four-thousandths of an ounce (0.1 g). But this is enough to kill more than 200,000 mice, or at least 50 people.

Tern, common

The **longest flights** regularly made by any bird species are made by the common tern during its annual migrations back and forth across the globe. One tern migrated from its breeding grounds in Finland to the east coast of Australia. The round-trip journey covered more than 32,500 miles (52,302 km), which the bird flew at an average distance of about 125 miles (201 km) per day.

Max length: 1 foot 2 inches
(36 cm)

Tt

Thread snake

Max length: 11 inches (28 cm)

The **smallest snake** of all is an extremely rare thread snake with the scientific name *Leptotyphlops bilineata*, which lives only on three small Caribbean islands. The smallest member of this species that has so far been found measured just 4¼ inches (10.8 cm) in length. Thread snakes spend nearly all their time burrowing underground in search of insect prey.

Fact
The sloth is not a primate and is only distantly related to apes and monkeys—its closest living relatives are anteaters and armadillos.

Three-toed sloth

Max length: 1 foot 8 inches (51 cm)

The world's **slowest-moving land mammal** is the three-toed sloth, from the tropical forests of South America. The sloth, also known as the ai, moves at a top speed of about 528 feet per hour (160 meters per hour) when traveling on the ground. When climbing through the branches, the animal can move nearly twice as fast as it can on the ground.

Max length: 10 feet
(3 m)

Tiger, Siberian

The tiger is the **largest of all the big cats**. The Siberian subspecies, also known as the Amur tiger or Manchurian tiger, is the biggest of them all. A full-grown wild male can measure 10 feet (3 m) from nose to tail, and weigh more than 850 pounds (385 kg). Siberian tigers held in captivity have grown even longer and heavier.

Max length: 2 feet 6 inches
(76 cm)

Trumpet conch

The world's **largest snail shell** is produced by a sea snail known as the trumpet conch, or baler conch. One found on the coast of Australia measured 2 feet 6 inches (76 cm) in length. This compares with a length of 10 inches (27 cm) for the largest shell produced by a land snail—the African giant snail.

Uu Vv

**Max length: 12 feet
(3.7 m)**

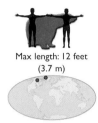

Ursus maritimus— Polar bear

Ursus maritimus is the scientific name of the world's **largest land predator**—the polar bear. The average adult male is about 8 feet 3 inches (2.4 m) long from nose to tail, and weighs about 1,100 pounds (500 kg). The largest polar bear on record measured 12 feet (3.7 m) in length and weighed 2,210 pounds (825 kg).

**Max length: 6 feet 6 inches
(2 m)**

Viper, Gaboon

Many venomous snakes use long, hollow fangs to inject their venom deep into their victims' bodies. The **longest teeth of any snake** are folded inside the jaws of the Gaboon viper, from western Africa. When this snake opens its mouth to strike, it reveals deadly fangs measuring up to 2 inches (5 cm) long.

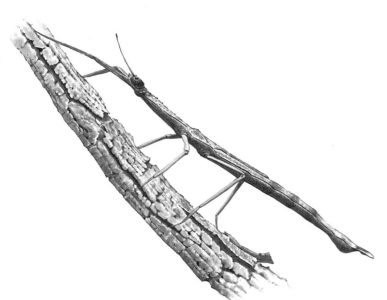

Walking stick

Max length: 11½ inches (29 cm)

The **longest insect** in the world is a species of walking stick (also known as a stick insect) from the tropical forests of Indonesia. With the scientific name *Pharnacia kirbyi*, this extreme insect has a body length of about 11½ inches (29 cm). Its long, thin legs can add another 8 inches (20 cm) to its total length.

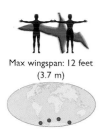

Fact

Walking sticks often make their natural camouflage even more realistic by "swaying" with the breeze, like real twigs.

Wandering albatross

Max wingspan: 12 feet (3.7 m)

The **biggest wingspan** of any bird is that of the wandering albatross, a sea bird that spends almost its entire life soaring above the Southern Ocean. The biggest wandering albatross ever accurately measured had a wingspan of 12 feet (3.7 m), although claims of up to 13 feet 10 inches (4.2 m) have been made for this species.

Ww

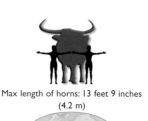

Max length of horns: 13 feet 9 inches
(4.2 m)

Water buffalo

The **biggest pair of horns** on any animal are those of the Asian water buffalo. The horns of one water buffalo from India were 13 feet 9 inches (4.2 m) from tip to tip. This is over 3 feet (91 cm) longer than the longest horns of any domesticated "longhorn" cattle.

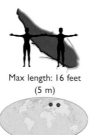

Max length: 16 feet
(5 m)

Wels

The **heaviest freshwater fish** ever caught was a wels, a European species of catfish, that was caught in southern Russia in the 19th century. This monster catch weighed more than 660 pounds (300 kg), and measured almost 16 feet (5 m) in length. Such huge catches are a thing of the past. Today, very few wels grow to be more than 6 feet (1.8 m) long.

Whale shark

Max length: 46 feet
(14 m)

The **largest fish in the world** is the whale shark, which can grow to more than 46 feet (14 m) long, and weigh more than 14 tons (tonnes). Despite its enormous size, the whale shark is a harmless monster that feeds near the ocean surface by filtering tiny plankton from the water.

Whistling swan

Max length: 4 feet 10 inches
(1.5 m)

No bird has **more feathers** than the whistling swan, which has an average of 25,000 feathers when full-grown. More than three-quarters of these are small feathers on the swan's head and neck. By comparison, some species of hummingbird have fewer than 1,000 feathers spread over their wings and body.

Xx
Yy

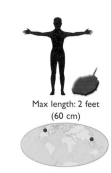

Max length: 2 feet
(60 cm)

Xiphosura

The strangest of all "**living fossils**" are the four species of horseshoe crab that live along the eastern coasts of Asia and North America. Horseshoe crabs, which are also known as king crabs, belong to the scientific group *Xiphosura*. Most members of the *Xiphosura* group became extinct about 400 million years ago.

Fact

Horseshoe crabs are only distantly related to modern crabs. Their closest living relatives are the bizarre seaspiders, which are not true spiders, just as the horseshoe crabs are not true crabs.

Yangtze River dolphin

Max length: 8 feet 3 inches (2.5 m)

The **rarest of all mammals that live in water** is the Yangtze River dolphin, which is also known as the baiji. This shy animal is found only in the lower part of one river in China. It has become critically endangered through hunting and water management projects, and there are now fewer than 100 Yangtze River dolphins remaining in the wild.

Yokohama chicken

The **longest feathers** on any bird in the world belong to the Yokohama chicken, which is also known as the phoenix fowl, a domesticated type of red jungle fowl that is bred in Japan for ornamental purposes. The tail feathers of one bird measured an incredible 34 feet 9 inches (10.6 m) in length.

Max length: 2 feet 8 inches (81 cm)

Zorilla

Max length: 1 foot 3 inches (38 cm)

The **smelliest animal** in the world is the zorilla from Africa, which is a relative of the American skunk. A zorilla can release a foul-smelling substance from special glands, which can be smelled more than a mile (1.6 km) away. This odor is strong enough to prevent even the hungriest lion from approaching a zorilla.

Glossary

Amphibian An air-breathing animal that lays jelly-covered eggs in water, such as frogs, toads, newts, and salamanders.

Antlers Branching, hornlike structures that grow from the heads of most deer. Antlers are shed and regrown every year.

Bat A flying mammal. Bats are true fliers that flap their wings, unlike flying squirrels that just glide. About one fifth of all mammal species are bats.

Bird A warm-blooded animal that has a body covered with feathers and lays hard-shelled eggs.

Bird of prey Any bird that hunts and eats other birds, mammals, reptiles, amphibians, or fish.

Camouflage Shape, color, and pattern that help an animal blend in with its background, so its enemies—and its prey—cannot see it easily.

Carnivorous Describes an animal that eats the flesh of mammals, birds, reptiles, amphibians, and fish.

Cold-blooded Describes an animal that relies on the environment to maintain its body temperature. Fish, amphibians, and reptiles are the major groups of cold-blooded animals.

Constrictor A type of snake that kills its prey by coiling tightly around its victim. This prevents the prey from breathing and causes death by suffocation.

Coral reef A rock-like structure just below the surface of the sea in coastal waters. Coral reefs have a surface layer of living coral animals, and are found only in tropical and subtropical regions.

Glossary

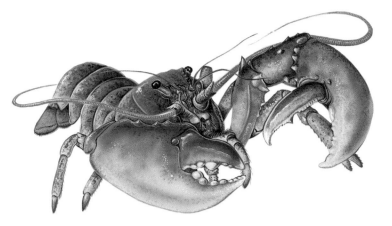

Crustacean An animal lacking an internal skeleton that is found almost exclusively in the sea. Crabs, shrimp, and lobsters are all crustaceans.

Domesticated Describes a species that was once wild, but has been changed into a different species after many hundreds of years as a farm animal or pet.

Endangered Describes a species that has such a small remaining population that it is in danger of becoming extinct.

Environment The surroundings in which a plant or animal exists.

Extinction A process by which a species ceases to exist when the last individual of that species dies.

Fang A long, sharp tooth designed for seizing prey. Many snakes have hollow fangs that inject venom when they bite.

Fish Water-living animals, most of which have a body covered with scales and breathe through gills.

Fresh water Rain water, river water, and the water in most lakes, is called fresh water because it contains no salt.

Gills The organs that fish, and some other water animals, use to breathe underwater. In most fish, the gills are visible as one or more slits on the sides of the head. Some amphibians have feathery gills on the outside of the head.

Gland A small organ that produces chemicals needed by an animal. Some animals have glands that produce toxins.

Glossary

Gravity The force that pulls everything toward the ground. Earth's gravity is responsible for objects having weight.

Insect A small animal with six legs and no internal skeleton. Many insect species also have wings.

Living fossil A species that has survived for many millions of years after similar species became extinct.

Lungs The organs (usually a pair) that mammals, birds, reptiles, and most amphibians use to breathe.

Mammal A warm-blooded animal that produces live-born young. Most mammals are covered with hair and live on land. There are a few aquatic mammals, such as seals and whales.

Migration Regular movement of animals from one place to another for feeding and breeding.

Mollusk One of a group of soft-bodied animals. Some mollusks, for example snails, make hard, protective shells for themselves. Another group of mollusks, which includes octopuses and squid, have no external shell, and are equipped with long, grasping tentacles.

Overfishing Catching so many fish that the total number of fish decreases every year. Some sharks and other fish are threatened by extinction because of overfishing.

Oxygen The chemical gas in air, which is essential for living things. Land animals take in oxygen directly from the air. Fish and most other sea creatures, take oxygen that is dissolved in sea water.

Plankton Tiny water animals and plants that range in size from microscopic to about one inch (2.5 cm) in length.

Predator An animal that hunts and eats other animals

Prey An animal that is hunted and eaten by others.

Primate One of a group of mainly tree-dwelling mammals that have the same basic body pattern as human beings.

Reptile An air breathing, cold-blooded animal with a backbone and scaly skin such as a snake, lizard, crocodile, or turtle.

Rodent One of a group of small mammals that includes, mice, rats, and squirrels, but not shrews or rabbits.

Savanna Tropical grassland with very few trees.

Scientific name Every species has a two-part scientific name written in the Latin language. For example, the polar bear is *Ursus maritimus.*

Shellfish A non-scientific term for invertebrate sea creatures that have a hard outer shell.

Species The particular scientific group to which an individual animal (or plant) belongs. Members of the same species all share the same characteristics.

Subspecies A group of animals belonging to the same species that differ slightly in color, size, or geographic location.

Toxin Any poison produced inside the body of a living thing.

Tropical Belonging to the geographical region around the Equator, between the Tropic of Cancer and the Tropic of Capricorn.

Venom A poison produced by an animal for the specific purpose of injuring another animal.

Index

A

Abingdon Island giant tortoise   8
African bush elephant   8
African Goliath frog   9
Anaconda   9
Arapaima   10
Asiatic elephant   10
Atlantic giant squid   11
Australian pelican   11

B

Bald eagle   12
Basketweave cusk-eel   12
Black mamba   12
Black-tailed prairie dog   13
Blue whale   13
Brazilian wandering spider   14
Brown rat   14

C

California condor   14
Capybara   15
Cheetah   15
Chimpanzee   16
Chinese giant salamander   16
Cuban frog   17

D

Dall's porpoise   17
Darwin's hawk moth   18
Deep-sea clam   18
Dragonfly, Australian   19
Dwarf lantern shark   19
Dwarf pygmy goby   19

E

Earthworm   20
Eastern lowland gorilla   20
Elephant seal   21
Emperor penguin   21
Etruscan shrew   21

F

Fairy fly   22
Flamingo   22
Flying fox, Bismarck   23
Forcipomyia   23

G

Galápagos tortoise   24
Garden snail   24
Geographer cone   25
Giraffe   25
Golden poison-arrow frog   26
Golden silk spider   26
Goliath beetle   27
Goliath bird-eating spider   27

H

Harlequin shrimp   28
Horned sungem   28
Howler monkey   29
Hummingbird   29

I

Icefish   30
Iguana, spiny-tailed   30
Illacme plenipes   31

J

Japanese spider crab   31
Javan rhinoceros   32

K

Katydid   32
Kitti's hog-nosed bat   32
Komodo dragon   33
Kori bustard   34

L

Least weasel   34
Leatherback turtle   35
Lungfish   35

M

Marion's tortoise   36
Mexican beaded lizard   36
Mexican free-tailed bat   37
Midgardia xandros   37
Monitor   38
Moose   38

N

Namaqua dwarf adder   39
North Atlantic lobster   39
Northern pygmy mouse   39

O

Ocean sunfish   40
Ostrich   40

P

Patu digua   41
Peafowl   41
Peregrine falcon   42
Piranha   42
Platypus   42
Poraque   43
Pronghorn   43
Pygmy mouse lemur   44

Q

Queen Alexandra's birdwing butterfly   44
Quelea, red-billed   44

R

Rattlesnake, eastern diamondback   45
Red kangaroo   45
Reticulated python   46
Rocky Mountain locust   46
Royal antelope   47
Ruppell's vulture   47

S

Sailfish   48
Saltwater crocodile   48
Sea dragon, leafy   49
Sperm whale   49
Spine-tailed swift   50
Sunspider   50

T

Taipan, inland   51
Tern, common   51
Thread snake   52
Three-toed sloth   52
Tiger, Siberian   53
Trumpet conch   53

U

Ursus maritimus—Polar bear   54

V

Viper, Gaboon   54

W

Walking stick   55
Wandering albatross   55
Water buffalo   56
Wels   56
Whale shark   57
Whistling swan   57

X

Xiphosura   58

Y

Yangtze River dolphin   58
Yokohama chicken   59

Z

Zorilla   59